realU®

GUIDE TO

PLANNING FOR COLLEGE

MAX OVERLY

Real U Guides

Publisher and CEO:
Steve Schultz

Editor-in-Chief:
Megan Stine

Art Director:
C.C. Krohne

Illustration:
Mike Strong

Production Manager:
Alice Todd

Editorial Assistants:
Cody O. Stine
Charles Bethea

Copy Editor:
Leslie Fears

Library of Congress Control Number: 2004090279

ISBN: 0-9744159-2-8

10 9 8 7 6 5 4 3 2

Published by
Real U, Inc.
2582 Centerville Rosebud Rd.
Loganville, GA 30052

www.realuguides.com

Real U is a registered trademark of Real U, Inc.

Photo Credits:
Cover and Page 1: Megan Stine. Page 3: Photodisc/Getty Images.
Page 4: Photodisc/Getty Images. Page 5: Girl by blue lockers,
Photodisc/Getty Images; Report card, Photodisc/Getty Images;
Locker room, ArtToday; Girl testing, Photodisc/Getty Images;
Piggy bank, ArtToday; Girl reading applications, Megan Stine;
Clock tower, Megan Stine. Page 6: Gothic campus building,
ArtToday; Girl on campus steps, ArtToday. Page 8: PNC/Getty
Images. Page 9: Girl in library, Nick Dolding/Getty Images; Teens
watching TV, E. Dygas/Getty Images. Page 11: Gen Nishino/Getty
Images. Page 12: Photodisc/Getty Images. Page 13: Stewart
Cohen/Getty Images. Page 14: Megan Stine. Page 15: Girl by lockers,
Photodisc/Getty Images; Squash racquet, ArtToday; Single pencil,
ArtToday. Page 16: Girl w/notebook, Megan Stine; Protractor,
ArtToday; Group at pyramid, Stewart Cohen/Stone/Getty Images.
Page 17: Students on campus, Doug Menuez/Getty Images;
Girl testing, Photodisc/Getty Images; Office meeting, ArtToday.
Page 18: Girl writing, Megan Stine; Teacher and students,
Photodisc/Getty Images; Girl in hat, Doug Menuez/Getty Images.
Page 19: Mother and teen girl, Megan Stine; Mail slot, ArtToday;
Signing check, ArtToday. Page 20: Photodisc/Getty Images.
Page 21: C Squared Studios/Getty Images. Page 22: Bandana girl
sitting, ArtToday; Blackboard writing, ArtToday; Anatomy textbook,
ArtToday; Girl reading on grass, Lawrence M. Sawyer/Getty Images.
Page 23: Arabic writing, ArtToday; Mom and girl, Jacobs Stock
Photography/Getty Images. Page 24: ArtToday. Page 25: Rubberball
Productions/Getty Images. Page 26: Boy and senior citizen,
Thinkstock/Getty Images; Soup kitchen, SW Productions/Getty
Images. Page 27: ArtToday. Page 28: Basketball game, ArtToday;
Campus walk, ArtToday. Page 29: ArtToday. Page 30:
Empty lecture hall, ArtToday; Campus clock tower, Doug
Menuez/Getty Images. Page 31: Girl in sundress, Jacobs Stock
Photography/Getty Images; Ivy-covered walls, ArtToday; Party scene,
ArtToday. Page 32: Observatory, ArtToday; Harpsichord, ArtToday.
Page 33: ArtToday. Page 34: ArtToday. Page 35: Girl in hat,
Doug Menuez/Getty Images; Hamburger, ArtToday. Page 36:
Classroom discussion, Manchan/Getty Images; Coach, Rubberball
Productions/Getty Images. Page 37: Stephen Simpson/Getty Images.
Page 38: Testing hall, Terry Williams/Getty Images; Hand writing
test, Photodisc/Getty Images. Page 39: Photodisc/Getty Images.
Page 40: Photodisc/Getty Images. Page 41: ArtToday. Page 42:
Photodisc/Getty Images. Page 43: ArtToday. Page 44: Megan Stine.
Page 46: Megan Stine. Page 47: ArtToday. Page 48: ArtToday.
Page 49: Megan Stine. Page 50: Manchan/Getty Images. Page 52:
Work study, ArtToday; Money background, ArtToday. Page 53:
ArtToday. Page 54: Money, ArtToday; Campus spire, Steve
Dunwell/Getty Images. Page 55: ArtToday. Page 56: Color wheel,
ArtToday; Paint brushes, ArtToday; Protractor, ArtToday. Page 57:
Girl in library, PNC/Getty Images. Page 58: ArtToday. Page 59:
Guy in letter jacket, Photodisc/Getty Images; Duct tape, ArtToday.
Page 60: Money, ArtToday; Piggy bank, ArtToday; Stock collage,
ArtToday. Page 61: Mark Andersen/Getty Images. Page 62: Steve
Schultz. Page 63: Doug Menuez/Getty Images; Back Cover:
Photodisc/Getty Images.

realU

GUIDE TO

PLANNING FOR COLLEGE

MAX OVERLY

GUIDE TO PLANNING FOR COLLEGE
TABLE OF CONTENTS

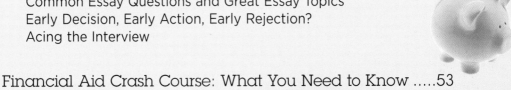

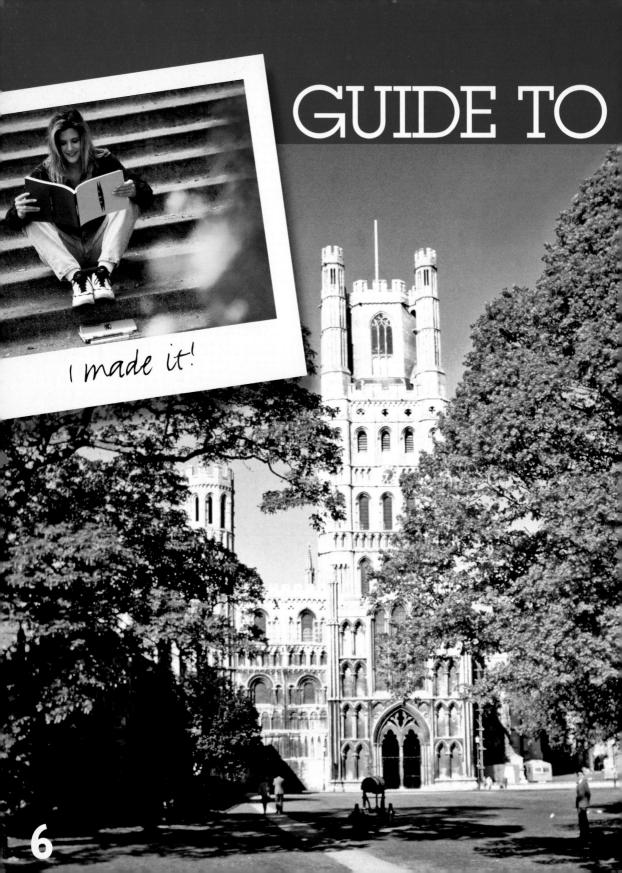

GUIDE TO

I made it!

PLANNING FOR COLLEGE

The Best Four Years of Your Life...

College. Talk about pressure.

It's not that you don't believe your friends, parents, and teachers when they tell you that college will be the best four years of your life. It's just that when your parents talk about how expensive it's going to be, and your teachers ramble on about how hard it's going to be, and your friends won't shut up about picking the perfect school, it seems like you might not survive long enough to *experience* the best four years of your life.

Bottom line: planning for college can seem harder than trying to hit on a member of the opposite sex the day after you've had your wisdom teeth removed. But take our word for it—hitting on a cutie when you've got chipmunk cheeks is much worse.

So turn the page and let Real U guide you step by step through picking the right colleges, filling out the applications, writing the perfect essays, interviewing at schools, navigating financial aid, and everything else you need to know about getting into the college that's right for you.

That's what Real U is all about. And good news—you can get into *this* university without passing a single test, writing a single essay, or filling out a single application.

Now all you have to worry about is those wisdom teeth. They are ready to come out, aren't they?

And welcome to

ARE YOU A COLLEGE PREP OVERACHIEVER?

Is planning for college likely to land you in a padded room before it lands you at Princeton?

Sure—just about everyone you know wants to go to college. But is everyone willing to jump through the same hoops to get there? Some of your friends are willing to ask their parents to proofread their college essays. (Probably a good idea.) Others are lining up to sell a kidney to an "admissions officer" in a hotel room somewhere outside of Boston. (Probably overkill.) Here's a quiz to help you figure out whether you're doing too little college prep, too much, or just the right amount.

starting early...

1.

First, the easy one. You started planning for college:

A. In Kindergarten, when your parents sewed Harvard pennants onto all your overalls.

B. In the second half of your freshman year—in high school, not college.

C. Right after you finished getting measured for your cap and gown.

your saturday night?

You're a high school sophomore. In an average week, how much time do you spend researching colleges?

2. You survived elementary school, middle school, and freshman year with minimal emotional scarring, and now you're a high school sophomore. In an average week, how much time do you spend researching colleges or thinking about how to improve your high school résumé?

A. All evening Monday through Friday, all day Saturday and Sunday, and all day and all night on holidays and snow days.

B. A couple hours, when your lousy good-for-nothing friends who said they'd be here an hour ago still haven't even picked up the stupid phone to call.

C. None—that's what senior year is for.

their saturday night!

9

3. You're in the admissions office at your top pick school, your fly is closed, and you haven't forgotten your own name or referred to the interviewer as "Big Guy" or "Tiger." In other words, the interview is going well! Then, out of left field, the admissions officer says, "So why do you think the Eastern New Jersey Institute of Veterinary Studies is right for you?" Not one to be easily shaken, you respond:

A. "When Dr. Peter Brown founded the New Jersey Institute of Veterinary Studies in 1483, he had a vision of a place where students from all races, creeds, and backgrounds could find a haven for the creative, caring, and individual spirit, a place where students and teachers worked in an atmosphere of harmony…"

B. "Well, this seems like a place where I could pursue my goals in a challenging but socially satisfying environment."

C. "For me? Ah, well...ahem...I did have a cat once...when I was younger. So...that's something. Right, Big Guy?"

4. It's time to sign up to take the SAT's. Your idea of SAT Test Prep is:

A. Shipping yourself off to a specialist in Zurich who claims to be able to increase your score by 750 points.

B. Calling a few friends over for the weekend to go over vocabulary lists and then doing a few practice tests.

C. Calling a few friends over for the weekend to see if any words from your vocabulary lists come up while watching a James Bond marathon. Then throwing darts at a few practice tests.

FAFSA???

5. FAFSA is:

A. A financial aid form, and your only friend.

B. Something you'll have to fill out later to help pay for college.

C. You don't know—but you think she must be one of the new freshmen.

SCORING

Here's some great news: the quiz you just took and the SAT are similar, in that they are both multiple choice. Think of this as an early practice test! That said, here's how to score the quiz:

IF YOU ANSWERED MOSTLY A'S:

You're ahead of the game, which is great. Just make sure you leave yourself a little room to relax. Remember, colleges like to know that you're interested in something—preferably something other than getting into college. Keep up the good work, but take a breather, and see if you remember any of your friends' names.

IF YOU ANSWERED MOSTLY B'S:

Congratulations. You seem to be balancing college apps and high school reality pretty well. If you keep up the good work, all your friends will be jealous, word will get around, and you'll be able to use your newfound popularity to achieve complete social and world domination. (Or at least get a date for Saturday night.)

IF YOU ANSWERED MOSTLY C'S:

Glad to hear that you're enjoying yourself in high school, but if you really want to go to college, it may be time to get into gear—and we don't mean reverse. Talk to your guidance counselor, your parents, or that friend who answered mostly A's and see if you can't get a few applications done during the commercials. Or better yet—turn the page and keep reading this book.

DECEMBER

PLANNING

FOR COLLEGE
Step by Step

No one is going to tell you that planning for college is easy or simple—at least, no one to whom you should lend your car keys.

But there is a pretty clear path between where you are now (on the couch, with your mouth hanging open) to where you want to be (in college, in your dorm, on the couch, with your mouth hanging open). And lucky for you, the first step doesn't even require that you get off the couch. The first step is to read this overview of the...

FIVE MORE-OR-LESS PAINLESS THINGS YOU SHOULD DO TO GET READY FOR COLLEGE

1. Get the best grades you can in High School.

2. Get the best scores you can on the SAT or ACT.

3. Get involved in extracurricular activities, to broaden your interests and show colleges that you're not spending all your time on the couch.

4. Pick colleges that are a good match for you—ones that offer programs you're interested in, and that suit your other needs and preferences.

5. Start early on the application process, so you can manage it with the least stress possible.

All you need now is a timeline telling you when to do these things. If only you knew where to find such a timeline...

TIMELINE:
PLANNING FOR COLLEGE

Theoretically, you could do everything you need to do to get into college during your senior year.

But unless you like quiet nights at home while the rest of your friends are out partying like—well, like they're seniors—then you might want to start a little earlier. Here's a step-by-step overview of what you should do each year in order to preserve the possibility of a senior-year social life. You'll thank us later.

PLAN OUT YOUR HIGH SCHOOL COURSES NOW.

That way, you can balance the challenging courses colleges like to see with those back-to-back study halls you've been planning for second semester senior year.

TAKE UP AN ACTIVITY.

Try squash (the sport, not the vegetable). Or football. Or knitting. If you get involved with extracurriculars now, by senior year your high school résumé will make you seem positively involved.

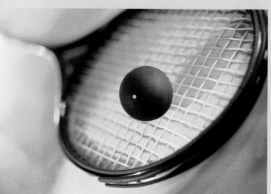

TAKE THE SAT II'S.

These test course-specific knowledge, and the more selective colleges require them. Best plan: take the test right after you finish the course. (The same goes for AP tests, if you're the Advanced Placement type, although you probably won't start taking AP courses until next year.) Follow this advice unless you think you'll still remember everything from Bio I when you're a senior...in which case you're kidding yourself.

TAKE THE PSAT.

Pretend the P stands for Practice. And guess what? The more times you take it, the better prepared you'll be for the real SAT. Taking the PSAT also puts you on college mailing lists.

START READING ABOUT COLLEGES.

It's not time yet for heavy-duty research, but it's never too soon to start thinking about what type of school you want to attend.

KEEP ADJUSTING YOUR HIGH SCHOOL CURRICULUM.

If you've discovered that you have a near-religious devotion to physics or literature or gym, re-plan your remaining high school courses to reveal this. Colleges like a HS transcript that shows your interests.

AGAIN WITH THE SAT II'S!

Keep up the good work.

DO SOMETHING USEFUL WITH YOUR SUMMER.

Like what? Get an interesting internship, or go to band camp. You can write your college essay about it later, and besides, those reruns of *Get Smart*! will still be on when you get out of college.

TAKE THE PSAT.

If you didn't do this last year, do it now.
If you did, do it again. The more testing, the better.

START MAKING LISTS OF SCHOOLS.

List schools that match your general preferences
and your academic or career goals.

START PLANNING CAMPUS VISITS.

Winter break, Spring break, and the summer after
Junior year are all good times to visit schools.
It's not too soon to set up campus interviews as well.

KEEP TAKING SAT II'S AND AP TESTS.

Strike while the iron is hot!

FIND OUT IF YOU NEED TO TAKE THE ACT.

Some colleges prefer this test, and some parts
of the country use it more frequently than the SAT.

SIGN UP FOR AN SAT OR ACT PREP COURSE, IF NECESSARY.

If your PSAT scores come back looking more like
a soccer score, it may be time to look for a course
to help improve your test-taking skills.

TAKE THE SAT (OR ACT)!

No more practice, this is the real deal. The earlier you
start taking the test, the more chances you'll have to take
it again (and again) if you botch it the first through seventh
times. The summer after junior year is a good time to start.

MORE SUMMER INTERNSHIPS.

Last summer's meaningful internship turned out to
be meaningful coffee-pouring? Try again this summer.

START WORKING ON YOUR RÉSUMÉ.

Pretty paper not required (yet). Think more along
the lines of how to frame your HS career as
something Mother Teresa would be proud of.

17

SENIOR YEAR

AUGUST:
MAKE YOUR FINAL LIST OF COLLEGES

AUGUST/EARLY SEPTEMBER:
GET ALL THE APPLICATIONS YOU NEED.
You'll have to send away for some of these,
so do this at the very beginning of the year.

OCTOBER:
SEND OUT EARLY DECISION
AND EARLY ACTION APPLICATIONS.
You'll need to do everything early, including getting
teacher recommendations, if you apply now.

NOVEMBER:
THE SOONER THE BETTER
Send applications to schools with rolling admissions.
Think November if you can swing it.

GET TEACHER RECOMMENDATIONS.
Talk to your teachers early about writing
recommendations. Hit them up for this before
everyone else does. Most teachers spend more
time on the first recommendation they write
than on the sixty-first.

WRITE YOUR ESSAYS.
Talk a teacher into proofreading them for you.

NOVEMBER/DECEMBER:
LAST CHANCE SAT'S.
If you're still not happy with your test scores, this fall is
your last chance (and the last time we'll mention it).

DECEMBER:
MAIL EVERYTHING TO SCHOOLS.

This means transcripts, test scores, applications, essays, recommendations, your ex-girlfriend—everything.

START WORKING ON FAFSA WITH YOUR PARENTS.

JANUARY:
SUBMIT FAFSA.

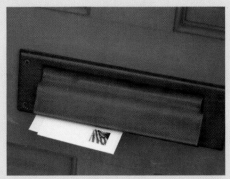

JANUARY—APRIL:
ACCEPTANCE LETTERS WILL START ROLLING IN.

Most schools notify in April unless they have rolling admissions, in which case you'll hear sooner. If you've been wait-listed, now's your chance to write letters to the admissions office telling them you're still interested.

MAY:
DEADLINE FOR MAKING YOUR DECISION AND SHELLING OUT CASH.

Once you've picked your school, you'll have to put in a deposit to hold your place (unless you're taking a year off). But you can keep looking around for aid packages and scholarships for the next several months.

YOUR HIGH SCHOOL

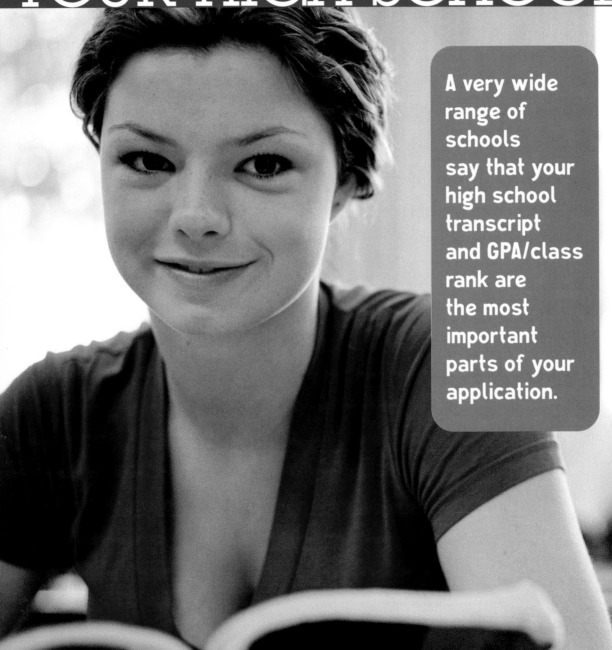

A very wide range of schools say that your high school transcript and GPA/class rank are the most important parts of your application.

How Colleges See It

If you think getting into college is just about applications, essays, and test scores, think again.

Most selective colleges consider a number of things when deciding whom to admit and whom to scrap, such as:

- Your HS transcript
- Your GPA and class rank
- Your SAT and other test scores
- Your essay
- Your extracurricular activities, special talents, and "personal qualities"
- Recommendations
- Alumni relationships
- Ethnic or racial background

And the list goes on. Every school ranks the importance of these things differently, but a very wide range of schools — from the huge state universities to the uber-selective Ivy League — say that your high school transcript and GPA/class rank are the most important parts of your application.

The fact is that hundreds of thousands of students are going to get the exact same test scores as you, and write fabulous, life-changing essays, and get personal recommendations from Jimmy Carter, and the only way colleges will ever be able to choose one applicant over another involves blindfolds and a dartboard.

But wait! If you start building your résumé now by selecting the right high school curriculum, you can make that personal recommendation from President Carter look like so much icing on the "cake" of your application (this is getting messy). Here are some tips and strategies to help make you stick out like a sore thumb on the "hand" of college admissions, as it were.

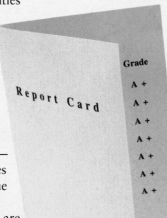

Report Card

Grade
A +
A +
A +
A +
A +
A +
A +

THE BALANCE GAME

Highly selective colleges prefer applicants who have taken the "most demanding curriculum offered" by their high school. They also like to see students who have high GPA's, and who finished in the top 5 or 10 percent of their class. On the other hand, less selective colleges don't care if you've taken AP courses, but will still consider your GPA and class rank.

This means that if you're aiming for the top schools, you have to figure out how to give yourself a challenging curriculum but still stay on top of it and get good grades. Ask yourself honestly how much work you can handle, and then pick your courses accordingly.

If you're aiming for a less selective school, however, you may want to bypass the toughest high school courses, and just make sure you've got a workload that allows you to keep your grades up.

ALL IN THE TIMING

If you're going to take some tough courses, a good way to keep your schedule balanced is to space them out over the four years of high school. If you know you're going to take three AP courses, for instance, don't wait until second semester of your junior year to sign up for them. Get some out of the way early so that when application season rolls around, you don't have to worry about a ridiculous course load.

YOUR GUIDANCE COUNSELOR IS YOUR FRIEND

How do you know what courses colleges want to see on your transcript? Ask your guidance counselor. How does he or she know? Guidance counselors communicate directly with admissions offices about their high school curricula, and many applications (including the Common Application) have a special section for guidance counselors to fill out about your high school career and course load. (If you've never heard of the Common App, see the box on page 46.)

ELECTIVE CHALLENGES

Taking AP and Honors classes isn't the only way to make your high school transcript look good. Colleges get excited when they see that you've taken advantage of elective periods to broaden your academic interests. But again—try to stay focused on the big picture. If you need that free period in order to keep your physics grade up, take it. But if your most challenging required

I got three A's!

course this semester is advanced candle-making, you'd better sign up for an extra foreign language, a journalism class, or another writing-oriented course. These are the kinds of electives that schools like to see. And besides, they'll set you ahead of the pack with skills you'll need when you get to college—skills like writing essays, or hitting on foreign students.

YOUR GUIDANCE COUNSELOR IS STILL YOUR FRIEND

Let's say everything's going well, and you've got a transcript that makes it look like your teachers only learned the first letter of the alphabet. Then senior year you get hit with a particularly brutal teacher who gives nothing but B's and C's to everyone in his class, just out of the goodness of his heart. Here's another chance for you to communicate with your guidance counselor, and your counselor to communicate with your colleges about this lower grade. Schools are often willing to take into consideration the fact that your B- from Dr. Pain is equivalent to an A from anyone else, if your counselor says so.

"RISING TRENDS" AND "FALLING TRENDS"

These are the terms colleges use to describe transcripts that show improvement or deterioration over the whole four years of high school. "Rising trends," in which mediocre grades steadily get better as you get older, are viewed more favorably than "falling trends," in which it becomes obvious that after freshman year you started slacking off. This is good news if you got off to a rocky start when you first entered high school—colleges can assume from your "rising trend" that you simply became more mature as you went through high school, or perhaps that you had a secret and highly experimental operation to improve your IQ by 50 points. But remember that "falling trends" can significantly decrease your chances of admission to the most selective schools, so it's important not to indulge in slacking or "senioritis," especially when you're, say, a junior.

If you're aiming for the top schools, you have to figure out how to give yourself a challenging curriculum but still stay on top of it and get good grades.

All About

Extracurriculars

Do colleges really care what you're doing after school?

Here's the simple truth about extra-curricular activities and your college application: many state schools are just too big, and receive too many applications each year, to care what you've been doing in your free time.

But for many smaller schools—and for the most selective colleges—this is an important element on your high school résumé. It's also a subject about which admissions officers have been more fickle than the judges on a reality TV show.

For years, colleges said they wanted nothing but "well-rounded" applicants: the star-quarterback-newspaper-editor-who-loves-children-and-plays-the-oboe type. But over the past couple of years, the balance has shifted toward what admissions offices are calling "well-lopsided" students: the really-really-really-really-loves-to-play-the-oboe type.

So what do you do while waiting for colleges to make up their minds? We recommend this somewhat revolutionary strategy: pursue your interests. If you join the yearbook and find that writing funny picture captions is your life's calling, then go for it. Put in the hours,

try out for editor, win some awards for your school, and colleges won't necessarily mind that you didn't also join the rugby team.

But if being well-rounded comes naturally to you, colleges aren't going to penalize you—as long as you don't overload yourself so much that your grades suffer, or you're unable to excel at anything.

The key is that the most selective colleges like to see students who demonstrate

internship at the senior center

INTERNSHIPS

Good summer internships can become the crowning achievement of your extracurricular résumé—especially if your love of the oboe is starting to seem unrequited.

Many students do volunteer internships with non-profit organizations. (In fact, a lot of high schools require some sort of service internship.) Working at the local soup kitchen or food bank can be a great way to show colleges your involvement in the community. And the wealth of experience you'll get doing an internship like that can be great material for your application essays. After all, it's much easier to write about the meaningful experience you had helping the homeless or working as a page in your state legislature than the meaningful experience you had trying to find some change you think may have fallen between your parents' couch cushions.

leadership skills and an ability to get involved in their communities. These are the students who tend to continue their tradition of leadership and involvement once they enroll in college—and if there's one phrase that'll make an admissions officer's mouth water every time, it's "tradition of leadership and involvement."

In addition to public service, you might also seek out a vocational internship, which can be a great way to get more involved in the field you're interested in.

If you're having trouble finding an internship, there are a bunch of resources available that list every internship imaginable by location and type. Check out www.realuguides.com for more info.

Oh, and did we mention that doing an internship may actually make you into a more well-rounded person, not just help beef up your résumé? That's good, too.

EVERYONE'S DOING IT:
PICKING THE BEST EXTRACURRICULARS

Here are some of the extracurricular activities that selective colleges particularly like to see on your résumé—especially if you excel at them:

- **Debate**
  National Forensics League, etc.

- **Government Internships**
  Senate Page, etc.

- **National Honor Society/Key Club**

- **Entrepreneurial or Business Ventures**
  Good luck.

- **Journalism**
  Particularly editor-in-chief or section editor positions.

- **Other fine arts**
  Includes visual arts, theater, and dance. But competition is tough, so it helps to be regionally or nationally recognized.

- **Working a part-time job during the school year**
  If you can manage this without hurting your grades, colleges will be impressed by your multi-tasking skills. In this case, it doesn't matter what kind of job you have, but if you find something in a field that interests you, go for it. Colleges will be doubly impressed.

- **Some Musical Instruments**
  It's a plus if you play one of the lesser-played instruments, such as contrabass, oboe, bassoon, or harp.

Here are some extracurricular activities which may not be impressive to colleges, and why:

- **Student Government**
  This is often more a popularity contest than a test of leadership. For student government positions to be viewed positively, you have to show that your student government is actually involved in the community, and did something more than plan the after-prom party.

- **Other Musical Instruments**
  You don't get many points for playing one of the most common instruments, such as piano, violin, or alto saxophone. Colleges receive thousands of applications from qualified musicians on these instruments. To stand out in the crowd, you'll have to have some regional or national recognition for your talent, such as concerto contest wins or selection in a prestigious national youth orchestra.

bassoon good, piano bad

27

great basketball team!

CHOOSING THE RIGHT SCHOOL FOR YOU

If you're like a lot of people, you're probably planning to put aside about twenty minutes during your junior year to draw up a list of the schools you'll apply to next year.

A nd while you're at it, maybe you'll spend half an hour learning brain surgery, and a few days writing the Great American Novel, too. Right?

Yeah. That didn't work when we tried it either. Turns out, narrowing a list of thousands of colleges down to a manageable five or six or seven might take you a bit longer than twenty minutes. But there's no reason to feel overwhelmed, either. Sure—there may be more than 300 desirable schools in the country, but lucky for you, about 290 of them won't be right for you in one way or another. Here are some quick and easy ways to narrow the field.

the lecture halls here are huge!

BIG OR SMALL

Colleges range in size from more-friends-than-you-had-in-third-grade to more-friends-than-you'll-ever-want-to-have, and this is one of the easiest ways to thin the pack. Like getting lost in the crowd? Big is probably the way to go. Big schools often have other advantages, too —they generally offer more extracurricular opportunities than smaller schools, and often have a wider range of majors. On the other hand, small schools tend to offer smaller class sizes, which means more direct contact with your professors. And on a small campus, you pretty much get to know everyone by name. Anyone for tea with the Dean?

HERE OR THERE

There are two reasons to think about going to a school in your home state. First, you may simply want to stay close to home. College is supposed to be an adventure, but there's still no substitute for getting your mom to do your laundry. Second, state schools (as opposed to private schools) almost always offer significantly lower tuition for in-state residents—leaving you with more cash to get your bling-bling on, or, failing that, for pizza.

URBAN, SUBURBAN, OR CAN-ANYONE-SAY-*SURVIVOR*?

Setting is another easy way to pick your school. Urban colleges have the advantage of providing the excitement and opportunities of the big city, but they often lack a central campus, or much feel of campus life.

There are exceptions to this rule: some urban schools have an enclosed campus, with dorms and classroom buildings arranged around a central green. This may be the best of both worlds if you're a big city lover who wants a good campus life. But big cities can also be a bit distracting when your favorite band comes to town the night before your organic chemistry midterm is due. Small town schools, on the other hand, offer the classic college town experience —but expect life to be focused mainly on campus and a few local town hang-outs. On the far end of the spectrum, you'll find small, remote, rural schools. These can be pretty isolated—often you have to drive a few miles to reach the nearest town, and don't expect to find much when you get there. But these rural colleges often make up for it by having

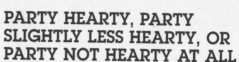

a vibrant campus life, or a particularly beautiful campus. With the social life so focused on campus, it may be easier to make friends and meet people than in more urban environments. But then again, you may end up alone, reading Milton aloud to the local population (which can tend to consist primarily of cows).

SUN-AND-FUN OR SNOW, MISERY, AND DESPAIR

In North Dakota it gets very cold. In Florida, not so much. Some people like a good blizzard.

GREEKS OR NOT

Seen Animal House? Like it? That's what the fraternity/sorority scene used to look like, and much of the party atmosphere remains on Fraternity Row to this day. But Greek life can also be about making connections with your peers for networking purposes, and these days some fraternities and sororities insist on making a positive contribution to the community by doing public service volunteer work. Greek houses can also provide an alternative to dorm life, although it may turn out to be a rowdy alternative.

PARTY HEARTY, PARTY SLIGHTLY LESS HEARTY, OR PARTY NOT HEARTY AT ALL

Colleges often have a reputation based on the relative raunchiness of their party scenes—or the nonexistence thereof. As you might guess, this often goes hand in hand with alcohol use, although not always. Some schools offer "dry campuses," on which all alcohol use is forbidden. Some colleges have fairly permissive alcohol policies, but not a very hard-core party scene. And even some "dry campuses" have a bit of a seedy underbelly.

the party scene....

31

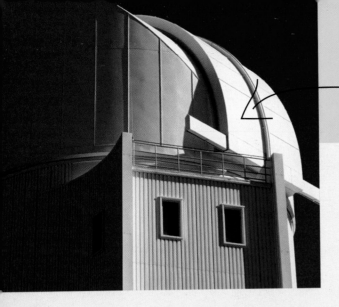

this school has its own observatory!

Of course, the official policy is not always a true indicator of what's really happening—but with a few exceptions, you can tell a lot about the social life at a school based on its policy toward parties. So try to figure out what kind of social life you want, and then choose your poison.

MAJORS OFFERED

Not every high school student knows what he/she wants to study in college. (Frankly, most college students take a while to figure it out, too, and some of them graduate without ever really being sure.) But if you do know what major or concentration you'll want to pursue, you should try to pick schools that offer a good program in your field.

SAFETIES AND STRETCH SCHOOLS

This one is less about preferences and more about applying to a well-balanced mix of schools. You'll want to pick one "safety school"—a school to which you know you'll be accepted. You'll also probably end up picking a few "stretch schools," where you very well may not get in. Middle schools, where your guess is as good as ours, will make up the rest of your list.

CHEAP AND EASY OR SOUL-CRUSHINGLY EXPENSIVE

We're listing this issue last, because the common wisdom in the college counseling business is that you shouldn't consider cost when you're making your first list of schools. The theory goes that if you really want to go to an expensive school, financial aid will make it possible, and having the perfect college experience will make it worth it. But in reality, your family may need to consider cost when picking a school, and you may want to consider how much debt you'll be saddled with if you have to take out massive student loans. Talk to your parents now to figure out how you're going to handle the financial situation—better now than later, so you can make sure you don't apply exclusively to schools that will be difficult to pay for.

GETTING YOUR NAME ON
DESIRABLE MAILING LISTS

The easiest way to get information about colleges is to get them to send it to you. How? One way is simply to take the PSAT. Make sure you bubble in your address correctly (no fake names, please), and you'll automatically be put on the mailing lists of a whole lot of schools.

But what if you aren't taking the PSAT? Or you took it, and were somehow overlooked? You can also request information two other ways: either directly from schools' web sites, or by making a call to their admissions offices. Get started early, though—it often takes admissions offices several weeks or even months to process requests for information, particularly during the busy fall admissions season.

THE QUEST FOR INFORMATION

The main marketing tool admissions offices send out is the "viewbook," a glossy brochure with basic promotional information about the college. This is a great way to get a first look at a college you're interested in. But if you want to get past the PR view of any given school, ask for more information. Particularly useful, if somewhat daunting, are the thick college catalogues published by many schools. These list courses offered, professors and department heads, majors offered, and lots of other information about what's required to get a degree. You can also go to www.realuguides.com for our recommendations on the best college guide books and college info websites.

Once you've read all the printed stuff, you'll want to plan visits to the schools you're considering. Read on!

33

STORMING THE GATES:

8 TIPS FOR VISITING COLLEGES LIKE YOU KNOW WHAT YOU'RE DOING

There are a couple different ways to visit colleges.

In one scenario, you obediently follow a student tour guide in the rain during a tour which includes such highlights as The Architectural History of the Main Dining Hall. You probably don't have time to get in any questions, because some other kid's parents are busy reminiscing about the happy years they spent here, while their kid tries his best to disappear completely under the brim of his New England Patriots hat. Soaked to the bone by what has now turned into a Class Four hurricane, you return to the admissions office, where you pick up an application and go on your merry way.

The good news about this method is that you did two things right: you took the tour, and you picked up an application. The bad news is that you did everything else wrong. Here are eight tips for getting the most out of college visits.

taking the campus tour

1.
DO YOUR HOMEWORK.
Make sure you've read the brochures and other college publications before your visit, and then take some time to think about questions you might want answered while you're there. This works much better than making the visit first and then thinking about questions you could have asked later.

2.
TAKE THE TOUR.
College tours tend to be padded with a fair amount of promotional information you don't need, but they are also the best, quickest way to learn some basic facts about the college, and save you the trouble of being alone while wandering aimlessly across a campus the size of the former Soviet Union. On the tour, you'll be following someone else who is leading you aimlessly across a campus the size of the former Soviet Union. Huzzah.

3.
TAKE OVER THE TOUR.
Don't worry about offending the tour guide —or anyone else for that matter—by asking too many questions. Be assertive! Be ruthless! Play hardball! If the tour guide is cute, flirt shamelessly! See Page 37 for a list of good questions to ask.

4.
TRY THE FOOD.
Sure, you tell yourself that when you go to college, you're going to learn to cook for yourself, or possibly room with a French chef, and you'll never have to go near the campus dining halls. But in reality, your most elaborate attempts at cooking will involve ramen noodles and a hot pot, and your French chef, disgusted by your dorm room living conditions, will transfer to off-campus housing less than halfway through the first semester, and you'll end up at the dining hall every day for the next four years. Enough said?

5.

SCHEDULE AN INTERVIEW (IF THE SCHOOL OFFERS THEM).

Do this whether you're planning to apply to this school or not. If you end up applying later, you'll already have the interview out of the way. If you don't end up applying, you'll get to practice interviewing, which means you'll get more comfortable talking about how great you are for half an hour—as if that would be difficult for you. Remember to schedule well in advance, as inteview slots fill up quickly at many schools.

6.

GET TO KNOW THE PEOPLE.

Surveys show that a majority (almost 54%) of college students don't bite random strangers. So strike up conversations with students, no matter what it takes. This is absolutely the best way to find out what it's really like to go to the college you're visiting. Hint: our suggested questions for tour guides (on Page 37) will work on regular students, too.

7.

MAKE APPOINTMENTS WITH PROFESSORS, COACHES, GROUNDSKEEPERS, EVERYONE!

If your application is going to rely in part on any of your special talents—sports, fine arts, precocious academic specialization or other extracurricular achievements—you'll definitely want to "touch base" with the baseball coach, "get in tune" with the oboe professor, and, um, "get to know" the biblical studies department head. Call the office of admissions in advance to find out how you can get in touch with the right college faculty and staff.

the tour was excellent!

8.

RAID THE ADMISSIONS OFFICE'S SHELVES.

Take an application so you won't have to send away for one later. Then take a course catalogue, some brochures, a copy of the campus newspaper, a copy of the literary magazine, a few nice desk chairs, and a set of filing cabinets. (Okay, maybe not the furniture.) All of these things will help remind you which college was which when, later this fall, they all start to blend together into something like a dream sequence from a 1960's psychedelic film.

QUESTIONS TO ASK YOUR TOUR GUIDE

The best way to get straight answers out of your tour guide is to ask specific questions about his or her experience, rather than general questions about the whole student body. Here are some examples:

- Do you like your professors/classes?
- Do you have a lot of contact with professors?
- What's your average workload?
- What do you do for fun around here?
- How often do you party or go out?
- Do students date?
- Are you doing anything on Saturday night?
- Are you (and your friends) generally happy?
- What about drug and alcohol use?
- How's the food?
- How are the dorms?
- Is the weather always this lousy/fantastic/mediocre?
- Is the school well-run, or is there a lot of red tape?

Call the office of admissions in advance to find out how you can get in touch with college faculty and staff.

Remember that the SAT can be a bit more challenging than the PSAT.

SAT's and More

Taking these tests may be the most stressful part of the college application process, particularly if you still haven't conquered your strangely Freudian terror of No. 2 pencils.

For those of you who tuned in late, the SAT and ACT are standardized tests administered to high school juniors and seniors across the country—the SAT primarily to students on the two coasts, the ACT primarily to students in the Midwest—and required by almost every college.

Although there are significant differences between the SAT and the ACT, you'll take one or the other, and they are interchangeable in the eyes of most admissions offices.

Taking these tests may be the most stressful part of the college application process. But thanks to a little practice and some clever test prep, millions of students walk away from standardized tests under their own power each year. And if you follow our tips for test prep, you too can avoid being carried out on a stretcher, moaning, "APEX is to NADIR as 800 is to MY SAT VERBAL SCORE."

SIGNING UP

The SAT and ACT are administered several times throughout the year, at thousands of testing sites around the country. If you go to a big school, it may be that the test is offered right at your school. Otherwise, you'll have to sign up to take it somewhere else in your area. We've got advice later in this chapter on when you should take the tests, but no matter when you do it, you'll have to find the specific dates and locations of the tests from the College Board (SAT) or ACT, Inc. (ACT). You can sign up for these tests directly online at www.collegeboard.com and www.act.org.

ROUND 1
PRACTICE MAKES HALFWAY DECENT

TAKE THE PSAT

We thought the P stood for "Petulant," because that's how we felt after taking it. And a lot of people thought it stood for "Practice" or "Preliminary." Turns out, the P doesn't stand for anything these days, now that the SAT and PSAT have been officially renamed. (See Acronymophobia on Page 43) But thinking of this as a practice test isn't a bad idea, and taking this test is a great way to start practicing for the real SAT. Most schools offer it during your sophomore and junior year—why not try it both times? The scores will help you estimate how you're going to do on the real SAT. Taking the PSAT also enters you as a contestant for the National Merit Scholarship. Like your PSAT scores? Great. But remember that the SAT can be a bit more challenging than the PSAT, with harder vocabulary words and more advanced math.

THE PACT

O.K., there is no PACT, or Practice ACT. So if you are one of the (mostly Midwestern) students taking the ACT instead of the SAT, you'll have to administer practice tests to yourself. Read on.

MORE PRACTICE TESTS

No matter what test you're taking, doing more practice tests on your own is a great idea. If this is starting to sound repetitive, it's because repetitive practice testing is the best way to cut down on the stress of taking the test—and stress is one of the main reasons students have a hard time with standardized tests. You can get practice tests on the Internet, in books about testing, and often directly from the testing services themselves. Check out www.realuguides.com for more info.

WHEN TO PRACTICE

A week or two before your test date, set aside a few hours to complete an SAT or ACT practice test. This way the format of the test will be familiar and fresh in your mind when you take the actual test.

> You can save yourself time during the test by memorizing the instructions and familiarizing yourself with the format of the questions in advance.

ROUND 2
BRUTAL SELF-ANALYSIS

When your scores come back, evaluate whether you're happy with them. College guides often list the average scores of people who got into your top choice schools. Or, you can tell your friends your score and see if they give you a look like your cat just died.

If you're not happy with your scores, try to figure out what went wrong. There are three possible scenarios that may make you unhappy with your score.

DISASTER SCENARIO NO. 1: LOPSIDED SCORING DISASTER

Let's say you're acing the math, but you find the verbal section inscrutable and obtuse. Don't self-flagellate; your vituperation should be sublimated into amelioration of your testing aptitude. Or perhaps you knew all those words, but the math (or science on the ACT) gave you trouble. This is a common problem. It's possible that by working with your high school teachers, you can fill in the gaps in your test-taking skills without spending cash on a full-blown test prep program. Of course, test prep programs can help you with individual sections on a test, and if your teachers can't help you out, it may still be worth enrolling in a program. But if you did well on one section, you may already have the basic testing skills required to do well on the other. Maybe all you need is a little extra studying.

MEMORIZE THE INSTRUCTIONS

The SAT and ACT look the same every time you take them, so you can save yourself time during the test by memorizing the instructions and familiarizing yourself with the format of the questions in advance. Most test-prep coaches recommend this strategy —but make sure you're working with a practice test from the current year! Instructions and formats can change from year to year. Ah, if only the questions were the same every time...

BUBBLING TIPS FROM THE PROS

Test-prep professionals (yes, there are people who do this full time) recommend bubbling from the outside of the circle toward the middle. We suppose that's why they get paid the big bucks.

TAKE THE TEST

You should sign up to take the SAT or ACT during your junior year. That way, you'll have plenty of time for round two.

DISASTER SCENARIO NO. 2: TOTAL TESTING TRAIN WRECK DISASTER

Let's say you tell your friends your combined score and they think you're talking about your score for just one section. Hey—not everyone is good at taking standardized tests. It could be that you know your material but get stressed out when faced by the toothy grin of a half-bubbled answer sheet. Or it could be that the arbitrary format of the questions is throwing you off. If doing practice tests just reinforces your view of the SAT as your mortal enemy, and bubbling in answer sheets makes you break out in an embarrassing and difficult-to-explain rash, you're probably a good candidate for a test prep program. It will cut down on anxiety and help you master such useful life skills as analogies and quantitative comparisons. Some schools offer after-school test prep classes. Failing that, there are private companies, private tutors, and even online courses you can take to improve your overall test-taking skills. Go to www.realuguides.com for more info.

DISASTER SCENARIO NO. 3: OVERZEALOUS OVERTESTING DISASTER

Let's say your scores come back about 10 points short of perfect. A lot of high achieving students will want to take the test again, thinking it will be easy to pick up those last 10 points this time. Of course, this isn't really a disaster, but there are two possible problems with it. First: every score from every SAT you take will get sent to your colleges—not just your best scores. So if you take the test again and do worse, you're not helping yourself out. Second: relax! You're in good shape. Colleges will be more impressed if you spend that time doing volunteer work, rather than sitting through yet another standardized test.

If doing practice tests just reinforces your view of the SAT as your mortal enemy, you're probably a good candidate for a test prep program.

ACRONYMOPHOBIA

Anyone applying to college (or anyone writing a guide about applying to college, for that matter) may develop a case of acronymophobia: the fear of acronyms. Acronyms are abbreviations formed by the first letters of each word in a phrase—for instance SAT used to stand for Scholastic Aptitude Test. But in 1994, the College Board officially renamed the test the SAT I and stated that the name was no longer an acronym—the letters don't stand for anything.

Here's a quick glossary to help you decode the letters, and to tell you what's on the tests.

PSAT/NMSQT

Used to stand for Preliminary SAT/National Merit Scholarship Qualifying Test, and some people think the P stands for Practice SAT. Same format as the SAT, for obvious reasons.

SAT I

No longer an acronym, but this is the main test. Until 2005, it includes a Math and Verbal Section, the latter focusing on vocabulary. After 2005, SAT I will include more advanced Math (up through Algebra II, with some trigonometry, probability, and statistics), and a substantially revised Verbal section, which will focus on reading comprehension and writing skills, and will include an essay section. Almost all colleges require applicants to take either this one or...

ACT

American College Test. Usually taken by Midwestern students, but also used by various schools and colleges scattered nationwide. ACT is different from the SAT in that the ACT tests science reasoning as well math and verbal skills.

SAT II

Single subject tests. Many selective colleges often require that you take two or more of these and submit scores along with your SAT I scores. The SAT II Writing test is often required or recommended by selective schools, although this may change with the addition of a writing section to the SAT I.

AP

Advanced Placement tests, to accompany the advanced placement courses offered by your high school. Like the SAT II, each one tests your knowledge of a single subject. Score well on these and you can get college credit, and even opt out of some introductory college courses. At some colleges, students can opt out of a full semester's worth of courses, thus saving big bucks on tuition.

TOEFL

Test of English as a Foreign Language. Usually required for foreign students applying to American schools, although some elite institutions require foreign applicants to take the SAT II Writing test instead.

WHEN IT'S TIME

TO APPLY...

It had to happen sometime.

Sooner or later, the college shopping honeymoon was going to end, and it was just going to be you alone in a room with your parents' old manual typewriter (or a black pen) and a stack of applications on which rests your future happiness and, frankly, your worth as a human being. (At least, it's going to feel that way.)

But luckily, you've already done something right: you requested applications from colleges' websites or mailed in the application request forms from viewbooks months in advance, because you knew that admissions offices can take a long time to send these applications out. Or maybe you just went online, knowing that many colleges also offer online applications which can be submitted on the web. (Some also offer printable applications on their websites.)

So now you're ready to get to work. Lucky for you, we've gotten our hands dirty dissecting the application and identifying its parts, using the Common Application as our guide. (For more about the Common App, see the box on Page 46.) Now we're laying it all out on the table for you. Roll up your sleeves—here goes.

Personal And Educational Data

Print clearly in black ink, or type. Take a break. Have a sandwich.

Test Scores

Some applications (including the Common App) have a space for you to fill in your SAT, ACT, and SAT II scores, but don't kid yourself. This isn't an invitation to lie, cheat, exaggerate, or turn a 3 into an 8 in an effort to convince M.I.T. that you're a math genius. You'll still have to get the official scores sent in from the testing service. Your guidance counselor can do this for you, or you can call the testing service directly and have them send your scores to every school you're applying to.

Academic Honors and Extracurricular Activities

Often called the "short answer" section, this part of the application has recently become more important to admissions counselors, who grow weary sorting through more and more essays which overachievers have had edited by Pulitzer Prize-winning authors. Although this short-answer section often merely asks you to list your achievements, both academic and otherwise, it offers you yet another chance to talk about the more important (and most flattering) events of your recent life. Whether you use a list format or full sentences (some applications only leave space for a list), think about your answers carefully, and be sure to emphasize the stuff that really makes you stand out.

more about applications

THE COMMON APPLICATION

Used by hundreds of private universities and colleges, the Common Application is making the application process simpler by allowing students to fill out one application many times—or photocopy the same application—rather than requiring them to navigate dozens of different applications. Some schools accept only the Common Application. Others allow you to choose: use the Common App or their own application. Many schools accept the Common App if you submit it along with a special supplement published by the school. But all schools which offer the Common App as an option say that they don't distinguish between their own application and the Common Application at all—so do whichever feels right. You can find the Common App at www.commonapp.org.

Other Short Answers

Some applications include other short answer questions, but one of the most common is the ever-popular, "Why us?" in which you're asked to explain why you think this school is uniquely suited to your needs, and vice versa. The danger here is that if you simply recycle everything you learned about the school from its catalogue, the admissions office is going to notice. Yes, even if you swap some of the sentences around. For this reason, it pays to get personal. Talk about your real feelings about the school, or something memorable about your college visit, or some very specific career goal which you think this college will help you achieve.

Teacher Recommendations

You don't get to do anything with this except hand it over, and then bug your teachers to make sure it gets done. Some schools ask for two; some ask for one. All schools ask that recommendations be sent in a sealed envelope, separate from the rest of your application—sorry, no peeking.

School Recommendations or Report

This form gets sent along with your official high school transcript. It usually includes a section for you to fill out about your senior year courses (because they won't appear on your transcript until later) and a section for the guidance counselor to fill out about your class rank, how demanding your high school curriculum is, and other data about your school.

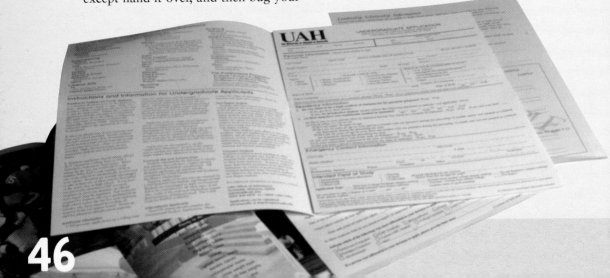

COMMON ESSAY QUESTIONS AND GREAT ANSWERS

One of the most legendary and frightening parts of the application is the essay, in which you're asked to write about five hundred words summing up your entire existence in terms that make you sound like a modern-day Mahatma Gandhi.

The essays serve two functions for admissions offices. First, they serve as the only real sample of your writing and thinking skills which colleges will get to see (until you turn in your first paper as a freshman). Second, essays give you a chance to tell colleges something they otherwise wouldn't know about you from the application—and preferably something more significant than how you stained your gray pants and why it made you a better person.

There are dozens of variations of essay questions and a million ways to approach them. Some essay questions call for very specific answers. For instance, the University of Chicago (famous for its coyly self-titled "Uncommon Application") changes its essay prompts every year, but in 2003, they offered one question which asked you to come up with a scientific theory explaining Non-Dairy Creamer, the Platypus, The End of Everything, Art, The College Rankings in U.S. News and World Report, or a number of other inscrutable phenomena. (Cute. Thanks, guys.)

Luckily, if you're not applying to the University of Chicago, you're much more likely to run into one of the Basic Three, which appear on the Common Application and just about everywhere else (including some bathroom walls):

1. Talk about an event in your life that affected you.

2. Talk about a person or book that influenced you.

3. Discuss an issue of local, national, or international importance and state why it matters to you.

There's no right way to answer these questions—in fact, the questions are so vague that sometimes it may seem like there's no way to answer them at all. But here are a few tips to get you started.

great tips

not a great essay topic

The easiest way to write a boring essay is to write what you think colleges want to hear.

Just Be Yourself

There's a reason they call it the "personal essay." The easiest way to write a boring essay is to write what you think colleges want to hear. Instead, think about the things you want colleges to know about you, and write about those.

Focus, Focus, Focus

It's better to pick a single specific event in your life, or a single encounter with the person or book that influenced you, than to list every influential event that's happened to you since you were three. The key here is making a choice and then sticking with it for five hundred words. If you pick something that really affected you, it ought to be easy to churn out a page and a half on it.

No One Cares About Your Student Government Association's Car-Wash Fundraiser

Same goes for your trip through the South of France, in which you realized how big the world is, but how we're all really the same. Surely you've done something which hasn't been done by every other high school senior in the country —how about writing about that?

Proofread Like Your Life Depends Upon It

Then get a teacher, parent, or the entire staff of the *New York Times* to do the same. If necessary, place a bounty on the head of the person who misses a typo.

Take Some Risks

Admissions officers read literally thousands of these things each year. At this point, they'll be grateful for anything that breaks up the monotony. Of course you should be careful about grammar and spelling, but you should also try to write in your own voice, or at least a voice that genuinely interests you—like, say, Ernest Hemingway's voice, or Jay-Z's (sans profanity, preferably). Same goes for picking topics. Perhaps the book that influenced you most is the phone book; perhaps the current event you comment on is Tuesday morning. Be creative.

EARLY DECISION, EARLY ACTION, EARLY REJECTION

For the overzealous, over-confident, and strong of heart, there are ways to make the college admissions deadlines come even sooner during your senior year, so that you can start weeping inconsolably a good four months before any of your friends when you don't get into Harvard!

Or, to put it differently, there's a way to cut down on stress in the second half of your senior year and get the whole college application process out of the way early, so you can start gloating intolerably a good four months before any of your friends when you do get into Harvard!

Either way you put it, it's called Early Decision or Early Action, and it's exactly that: early. As in, you apply early (at schools that offer one of these programs), and you get a response early. How early? You'll have to get Early Decision or Action applications in by early- or mid-November, instead of December, and you'll usually get an answer before the end of December, instead of April.

Here are the differences between Early Decision and Early Action.

EARLY DECISION

Early Decision is "binding," which means that when you turn in your early decision application, you're making a promise to attend that school if they accept you. You're also making a promise that, if you're accepted on Early Decision, you'll withdraw all your applications to other schools, to signal those other schools that you won't be attending. For this reason,

you can only apply Early Decision to one school.

There's another kind of Early Decision, sometimes called Early Decision 2 (we call it "Revenge of Early Decision"), offered by a few schools. This program lets you apply at the normal deadline but you get an answer earlier—usually in six weeks. Like Early Decision 1, this is binding. You have to go if you get in.

One drawback to Early Decision is that if you get in, you have committed to attending a certain school before you find out what kind of financial aid package they'll offer you. Since very few schools

49

ACING THE INTERVIEW

guarantee that they'll meet 100% of your financial need, this can be a serious problem if you intend to rely on financial aid.

EARLY ACTION

Early Action, by contrast, is laid-back, for laid-back hyper-organized over-achievers. You apply early and get a response early, but it's not binding. You can continue to apply to other schools, and matriculate wherever you want (as long as it's not on the rug).

BUT, I MEAN, REALLY, WHY BOTHER?

Early Decision and Early Action are best for students who are sure about their first choice school—very sure, in the case of Early Decision. As we said, finding out early whether you got in can be a remarkable stress-reliever. And if you don't get in early, you may still be admitted at the regular time, so you've got nothing to lose except that nonchalant pose you've been carefully cultivating for the last three and a half years.

At some schools, a higher percentage of applicants are admitted from the Early Decision and Early Action pool than from the regular admissions pool. This may be because the type of student who is organized and prepared enough to apply to college a month earlier than everyone else is simply more likely to get in. But on the off-chance that admissions officers are simply feeling cheerier early in the season, you might want to consider becoming one of those organized students yourself.

Bad news: we can't really tell you how to ace your interview. We just don't know you well enough yet. Fact is, if we told you to go in and talk about how much you enjoyed your band trip through Austria last year, when in fact your band went to Poland instead, you'd be lost, and our advice would be useless.

But here are a few general tips which should be useful no matter where your band went last year.

1. Early on in the application process, schedule an interview at a school that you don't want to attend—preferably at a school nearby. This is your practice interview.

2. Prepare answers to some common interview questions (see page 51) in advance.

3. Turn the tables on your interviewer by asking questions of your own—about the school, not about the interviewer, wiseguy.

This may make you feel more comfortable, and also shows the admissions officer that you're genuinely curious about the school. But...

4. Don't ask questions that could be easily answered by the college catalogue and brochures. Do your research first.

5. Feel free to take notes, or use notes you've prepared. Coming in with a court reporter is overkill. Coming with a few questions on a legal pad is excellent. Coming in with something scrawled on a bar napkin is just tacky, especially if it turns out to be someone's name and phone number.

6. Dress well, but don't overdress. A sport coat and tie are no longer necessary for men (although if a woman came in with a tie worn Rambo-style around her head, we would be amused, even if the admissions officer weren't). Nice pants, a dress shirt for men; skirt or nice slacks and a blouse for women. No ball gowns, please —this means you, too, guys.

7. Continue to be yourself. Think of the interview as an extension of the essay. You'll notice from our list of common interview questions that you'll often be asked the same question in interviews that you were asked in the essay, so be ready to talk on those subjects. But, also like the essay, be wary of giving answers that are "what they want to hear"—the best bet is to answer honestly, and try to project your real personality.

COMMON INTERVIEW QUESTIONS

Everyone's got a different interviewing style, but we'll be surprised if you don't run across a few of these:

- Why do you want to go to our school?

- Tell us about yourself.
  (See? Just like the personal essay.)

- Tell us about your high school and/or your high school experience.

- What questions can I answer for you?

- What are your goals for college and beyond?

- What are your strengths and weaknesses (a) as a student and/or college applicant, and (b) as a human being? (They won't put it this way, but watch out—they'll find a way to ask.)

- What three adjectives would you use to describe yourself—and the ever-popular variant, "What three adverbial clauses would you use to describe yourself?"

- What motivates you to succeed?

Finally, there is one trick question, which you shouldn't answer:

- What is your top choice school?

Unless you're interviewing at your top choice school, it's best to say that you're still thinking about it, or that you're keeping an open mind until you finish all your visits.

great work-study job

CRASH COURSE:
What You Need to Know

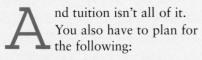

Perhaps you've heard that college is expensive. But really, how bad can it be, right? So you hop on the website of one of your favorite schools, check out the tuition, and—whoa, Nelly! College is bloody expensive!

And tuition isn't all of it. You also have to plan for the following:

- housing
- meal plans
- books and supplies
- pocket money for entertainment, coffee and snacks around finals
- travel to and from school
- activity fees, and so forth and so on.

So that's the bad news. The good news is that there are honey bunches of ways to pay for school, conveniently broken down into the following categories:

1. Financial aid
2. Scholarships
3. Saving and investing

Each one of these is a huge topic—more than we can cover in depth here. We'll give you an overview of the most important aspects of this subject, but eventually you'll want to check the Internet for more information. Some of the information changes rapidly, especially the government rules and regs for paying for college. Go to www.realuguides.com for our recommended links.

In the meantime, here's a look at typical college costs and a summary of the different ways to pay for college.

books are expensive!

COLLEGE EXPENSES

These are typical expenses, as of 2004, for one full school year (two semesters or three quarters).

	STATE COLLEGE OR UNIVERSITY	STATE SCHOOL	PRIVATE COLLEGE OR UNIVERSITY
	In-state residents	Out-of-state students	
TUITION	$4,000	$13,400	$28,600
ROOM AND BOARD	$7,000	$7,000	$9,000
BOOKS & SUPPLIES	$1,200	$1,200	$1,200
OTHER (Pocket Money, Laundry, etc.)	$1,200	$1,200	$1,200
TOTAL	**$13,400**	**$22,800**	**$40,000**

← can I afford it?

FINANCIAL AID

Whether you're looking for rancorous political squabbles or financial aid, the best place to start is always the Federal Government. Federal student aid comes in three handy sizes:

1. FEDERAL WORK STUDY

The federal government pays you to work a part-time job, usually at your school, in order to help you pay for tuition and other educational expenses.

2. FEDERAL GRANTS

These are based on financial need, and you don't have to pay them back.

3. FEDERAL LOANS

There are a few different types, and you will have to pay these back with interest.

Your "Financial Need" is the result of subtracting your Estimated Family Contribution (EFC) from the total cost of education.

FAFSA—THE FINANCIAL AID FORM

The good news about applying for all three types of federal aid is that you only have to fill out one form, one time: the Free Application for Federal Student Aid, or FAFSA. This gets submitted in January, after you've finished applying to all your schools. And no, you don't have to submit a FAFSA form to every school you applied to—you simply submit one form to the government, and they send it on to the colleges you want to attend. (See Other Forms for exceptions to this one-form one-time rule.)

What's on the FAFSA? Probably stuff you'll need your parents to fill out. It is essentially a financial profile of your family. You'll need to have last year's tax returns, your Social Security number (and your parents'), and occasionally

some other business reports, especially if your parents are self-employed. Be sure to get started early so that you have plenty of time to submit this stuff.

And then you wait. And then the government sends you and your colleges a Student Aid Report (SAR), which tells you your Estimated Family Contribution (EFC). This is used in a formula to calculate your Financial Need, which is used by the financial aid office at your college to determine your financial aid package.

A Note on Financial Need

Your "Financial Need" is the result of subtracting your EFC from the total cost of education. Since in theory your EFC remains constant, no matter what the cost of your chosen school, your

it all adds up!

Financial Need will change depending on tuition. For example, check out the following two hypothetical situations:

State school tuition & fees	**$7000**
Your EFC	**– $5000**
YOUR FINANCIAL NEED	**$2000**

Private school tuition & fees	**$30,000**
Your EFC	**– $5000**
YOUR FINANCIAL NEED	**$25,000**

In theory, then, it's not going to cost you more each year to go to Harvard than it would to go to Ohio State, because your Financial Need goes up as the tuition goes up—so you're supposed to be getting more financial aid to cover it. (Of course, it'll cost you more later,

when you're paying back your loans. But that's later.)

However, there are two possible problems with this theoretical system: the first is that many expensive schools don't use the FAFSA formula to calculate your Estimated Family Contribution—they make their own calculations, and guess what? They often come up with a higher EFC.

The second problem is that sometimes a financial aid office will offer you a package which does not meet your financial need. (You'll know this because the financial aid report will have a figure at the bottom titled "Unmet Need.") This means that either you'll have to raise your family contribution or go out and find more scholarships and grants if you want to attend this school.

OTHER FORMS

All right, we lied: sometimes you have to fill out more than one form to apply for financial aid. But it's not our fault, or the Federal Government's fault (for a change). Blame the colleges that require extra forms. Usually, it is the more expensive private schools which require these.

When you're applying for financial aid, be sure to contact the financial aid offices of every school to which you are applying in order to find out:

1. What forms are required, and

2. What the deadlines are for submitting those forms.

One form required by many schools is the PROFILE, which provides schools with a more detailed financial profile of your family.

Many schools also have their own FAFSA supplements, available from the financial aid office, which ask you specific questions not asked by FAFSA. These forms are every bit as important as FAFSA, so be sure to find out what's required and get it in on time.

WORK STUDY

If your financial aid package includes Federal Work Study money, it means that the federal government is offering to pay you to work during the school year, in order to help cover your tuition, room and board, and other expenses. This may be in addition to other grants and scholarship moneys, or it may be your only source of financial aid, depending on the financial aid package your college offers you.

Once you're notified that you're in the Work Study program, you'll have to apply for a Work Study job at your school. These jobs run the gamut—anything from washing pots in the dining hall to shelving books in the library or DJ-ing a shift on the college NPR-affiliate radio station. You'll generally have an hourly wage and get a biweekly or monthly paycheck just like you would at a regular job. One tip: since the good Work Study jobs (the ones that don't involve a hairnet) tend to fill up fast, apply early in the school year, so you can spend your hours far, far away from the dining hall kitchen.

FEDERAL PELL GRANTS

If your SAR tells you you're eligible for these, that's good news. Pell Grants are essentially like scholarships—they're free money, which you'll never have to pay back. However, unlike scholarships, which can often be based on your special talents or your racial or ethnic background, Pell Grants are based solely on your family's need, as calculated by the FAFSA formula.

FEDERAL LOANS

Federal loans also come in different sizes and shapes. Here are some basics:

■ Federal Perkins Loans

These allow you to borrow money at a low interest rate in order to pay for school. Perkins Loans are administered by individual colleges, so your eligibility for them will be determined in part by your financial need, but in part by the resources of the college. If, for example, another student applying for aid at the same college gets a big Perkins Loan, the financial aid office may decide not to award you as much money.

■ Stafford Loans

These also allow you to borrow money to pay for school, but they are awarded federally, not by individual schools.

■ PLUS Loans

These loans can be taken out by parents of undergraduate students to pay for undergraduate studies. Your parents are responsible for paying these back, and in order to qualify, they must pass a credit check. To get a PLUS Loan, your parents have to fill out a PLUS loan application, which they can get from the financial aid office at your college.

The term "Alternative Loans" refers to loans that are not federally subsidized. If your federal aid package still won't cover the cost of education, you can consider taking out a college loan from a private lender. These loans are often offered at higher rates, however, and many must be repaid while you're still in school.

SCHOLARSHIPS

Like federal grants, money stolen from the blind, and large gambling winnings, scholarships are free money. Huzzah! Also like gambling winnings, there are more ways to win scholarships than you can shake a stick at, but some of them are, well, shakier than others.

Luckily, there are a number of legitimate scholarship search services available online and through the mail. Visit www.realuguides.com for some recommendations. Some scholarships will even come directly to you without your having to search for them. But don't just sit there by the mailbox—read up on some basics while you're waiting.

Scam Scholarship Searches

Some scholarship search companies will send you direct mail offers "guaranteeing" that they'll find you scholarships "or your money back." Although some search services that contact you directly or require fees are legitimate, it's a good idea to check out any company before you fork over your cash. The Federal Trade Commission has a website with free information on scholarship scams at www.ftc.gov/scholarshipscams.

Go Local

Some of the best scholarship opportunities are right in your home town. Churches, synagogues, Rotary Clubs, and other non-profit organizations often have scholarship contests. Local newspapers will list scholarship opportunities, and often sponsor them, too. Bottom line: keep your eyes on the local scene. Since local contests draw from a smaller pool than national contests, even *you* have a fair chance of winning.

State Scholarships

Some states offer state-wide scholarship plans. These can be need-based or merit-based, but they are all generally for in-state residents attending state schools. Chances are that if your state has a program like this, you've heard of it, but ask your guidance counselor just in case.

Academic Scholarships

These can be awarded for academic achievement in a number of different fields, including the ever-popular National Merit Scholarship, which selects its semi-finalists based on PSAT scores. Even if you don't become a National Merit Finalist, many academic scholarships are offered by individual colleges to National Merit Semi-finalists and other high academic achievers.

Arts Scholarships

Sometimes offered by schools and sometimes by unaffiliated institutions, these can be tricky to come by, as competition is tough. For music scholarships, it helps if you play one of the lesser-played in-demand instruments.

Essay? Easy!

If you've ever read a book, chances are there's an essay contest with your name on it. If you haven't ever read a book, why not start now by reading Ayn Rand's *The Fountainhead*, one of many books for which there exists an essay contest? Top prize for an essay about that bruiser of a novel could win you five G's. That's about five bucks per page, come to think of it.

If you want to compete in the NCAA Division I or II, you'll have to register with the NCAA Initial Eligibility Clearinghouse, at www.ncaaclearinghouse.net.

Do an Internet search for "Fountainhead" and "Scholarship" to find out more. Or if you list "reading," "writing," or "literature" as your interests with one of the online scholarship search services, they'll come back with a long list of essay contests.

Sports Scholarships

Big bucks and "full ride" scholarships are difficult to come by, but many schools will offer you a small or partial scholarship if you excel at a particular sport. However, there are a few things every aspiring college athlete must do. First, build an athletic résumé which details your stats and accomplishments as an athlete. You'll send this out to coaches at the colleges where you're applying. Second, have someone videotape a number of your games, and be prepared to send these tapes to coaches. Third, if you

want to compete in the NCAA Division I or II, you'll have to register with the NCAA Initial Eligibility Clearinghouse, at www.ncaaclearinghouse.net. If you don't register for this, you won't be able to play NCAA sports, and if you can't play, you're not likely to get a scholarship. There are also all sorts of detailed rules about when college coaches can begin recruiting you or "courting" you, and how they can do it. You'll want to read about these rules on the NCAA website.

Ethnic Action

Thanks to colleges' desire to promote diverse campuses, you may qualify for scholarships simply based on your ethnic or racial background. Minority groups are always in demand, so be sure to indicate your ethnic background whenever you're participating in a scholarship search.

prom dress? —

STRANGE-BUT-TRUE SCHOLARSHIPS

Still haven't found a scholarship that fits your niche? Maybe you're the type who will qualify for one of these real, strange-but-true scholarships. Many of these are offered now or have been in the recent past.

- Left-handed people attending Juniata College in Huntington, PA. $1000.

- People who attend their senior prom dressed entirely in duct tape. Up to $2500.

- People who write "space music" or make "space art" inspired by space travel. Up to $1000.

- Catholics with the last name Zolp who are attending Loyola University in Chicago. Full four-year tuition.

- Female music students attending Depauw University who can sing or play the national anthem "with sincerity."

If your rendition of the national anthem still strikes most listeners as drolly ironic rather than sincere, try an Internet search with the word "scholarship" and just about any other search word, and see what you get.

SAVING AND INVESTING FOR COLLEGE

So you're a high school senior, and you want to think about saving for college. Great! Have any little brothers or sisters?

You have to get started a little earlier than now to save for yourself. But assuming that you've saved some money already, or that you're starting young, there are now a bunch of different ways to make your college fund work harder than ever before—harder than you're working at high school, anyway. So drag that wad of cash out from under the mattress and let us tell you where to put it.

State-run 529 Plans

State-run 529 Plans are probably the best thing to happen to college savings since, well, ever. Basically, you or your parents can set up a 529 Plan which allows your money to accrue interest tax-free. Yes, we said tax-free—as long as you're spending the money on higher educational expenses. (One catch: the tax-free provision is set to expire in 2010, unless Congress renews it. After that, you'll merely be guaranteed a reduced tax-rate on your earnings.)

State-run 529 Plans are probably the best thing to happen to college savings since, well, ever.

Another good thing about the 529 plans is that if you don't end up spending all your parents' cash on college, they can transfer the funds to another family member with no penalty.

As you might have guessed from the headline, these plans are offered by the states, but you don't have to use the one offered by your state if you find a better deal somewhere else. (For example, different states allow you to deposit smaller or larger amounts per year, and some states even offer tax deductible deposits.) For resources on picking a good 529 plan, check out the links at www.realuguides.com.

Independent 529 Plans

So far, only one company is offering this private 529 plan (see www.realuguides.com for more info), but it is another great way to save money for college. The private 529 plan works a little differently from the state plans. It allows you to pre-pay tuition at below-current rates, thus guaranteeing that you'll be able to pay tuition when the time comes. In other words, if $20,000 buys you one year at a selective school in the year 2004, you can invest less than that—something like $18,000 in 2004—which is then guaranteed to pay for tuition in 2008, even though by 2008 tuition may have gone up to almost $25,000. Good deal, right?

Coverdell ESA

Formerly known as the "education IRA," Coverdell ESA's—or Education Savings Accounts—are another way of investing for education. One bonus is that you can use the money for expenses related to elementary, middle school, high school, or college. Although contributions to a Coverdell ESA aren't tax-deductible, withdrawals of earnings are tax-free, like the 529 plan.

One problem is that not all families will qualify to put money in a Coverdell ESA. If your family earns more than a certain amount each year, the size of your contribution to the fund may be limited, or you may not be allowed to contribute at all.

no savings—gotta work!

YES!

First off, let's debunk one common college acceptance myth: small envelopes no longer mean you got scrapped.

We're not sure if this is because admissions officers started reading Miss Manners and realized they were using the wrong size stationery for personal correspondence, or if, somewhat more in character, they're just trying to mess with your head. Either way, you're going to have to open those envelopes before you start your embarrassing college admissions touchdown dance.

But after opening the envelope (watch for paper cuts), the hard part is over. All that's left now is to make a decision about where to go, and when. Ever helpful, we've got a few final tips for you.

FINANCIAL AID
If you're not happy with the financial aid package offered by your school, remember that you've still got time to look for scholarships or alternative loans before the fall. Also remember that you don't have to accept the financial aid package as is. If you want to take out smaller loans, or do less Work Study, that's an option. It may also be possible

ACCEPTANCE AND BEYOND

to negotiate with schools for more financial aid, particularly if you are a desirable or recruited student. Communicate with the office and tell them what you need. Hey, it can't hurt!

WORKING THE WAIT LIST

If you get wait-listed at your top-pick school, there are a few things you have to do. First, write a letter to the admissions office telling them you're still very interested. Think of this letter as a supplement to your application—in other words, feel free to include a few sentences about your recent achievements, and don't hesitate to tell the office why you still think their college is right for you. Second, this may be time to pull some strings, particularly if you have alumni

relatives or friends who would be willing to put in a good word on your behalf. But perhaps the most important thing you have to do if you're wait-listed is accept the reality: at highly selective schools, very few people are admitted from the wait list. The sad truth is that it may be time to think about your second choice.

ACCEPTED STUDENT DAYS

A lot of colleges offer special tour days for accepted students. Unlike the tour you took when you visited last fall, this tour is likely to include some useful information about things like applying for housing and choosing meal plans. You'll also have an opportunity to size up the rest of the incoming freshman, which may well be invaluable when you're making your final decision about which school to attend.

DEFERRAL

Taking a year off before enrolling in college can be a great way to avoid freshman burn-out, a common pheno-menon on today's college campuses. You've already been accepted, and simply spending a year in which you don't have to worry about college applications can do wonders for your state of mind. Can anyone say "Tahiti"?

MORE REAL U...

CHECK OUT THESE OTHER REAL U GUIDES!

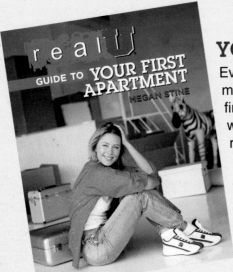

YOUR FIRST APARTMENT

Everything you need to know about moving out of the house and into your first apartment, including how to deal with landlords, how to dump your roommate, and much more!

IDENTITY THEFT

Find out how to protect yourself from the #1 crime in the U.S. Includes expert advice about surfing the Internet without leaving a trail for the criminals to follow. From the world-renowned identity theft expert and subject of the blockbuster motion picture *Catch Me If You Can*.

PLUS LIVING ON YOUR OWN

So you've finally moved into your first apartment. Now what? Plunge into real life with a safety net. If you can't cook, always shrink your socks, and have no idea where to find your stove's pilot light, this is the guide for you.

BUYING YOUR FIRST CAR

Don't get burned on the first big purchase you make. Find out how to get the best financing, how to avoid the latest scam tactics, whether to buy extended warranties, and more.